The House of I Am Mirrors

& Other Poems

The House of I Am Mirrors
& Other Poems

Bob Doto

New Old Traditions

Thank you to all who approach books as if they were a collection of spells. And, to Becky, for being wonderful in all ways, for taking the time to read whatever it is I'm working on, and for her many comments and feels.

First Edition: April 2021
Printed in the United States of America
ISBN-13: 978-0-578-88433-2

Cover design and layout by the author.

CONTENTS

For all who are caught in someone else's story.

The House of I Am Mirrors

A Great Mystery

1: Outside the Gates

There is not a place in this house
holding too tight.

Places the leg then the foot
then the key from its waist
in the house holds a new relic: a waste.

Sky-clad body for a bit with tools.

Fast arm.

A waist below a metal box goes
please turn me on.

I found a bone in the box & a home.

Once made my bed into a fort
made me think: home.

2: In the Foyer

The house is not yet the performance.

Peopled the unclear edges.

The difference between: open heart surgery
&: surging open heart

The guest introduced itself masked,
then masked & introduces itself again.

In the foyer is why not you make millions.

I make millions made me into my self.

I'm a merger.

& introduces me to its friend.

3: In the Big Room

Arrive (or I've been here before)
in an elevator
& you can tell I'm smiling at you
told me about it.

Across (or I've seen you before)
can we tell me about it?

Take bubbles. Take the next bubbles
spilt on the floor of my sweaty palms.

Silly mes all bubbling up against mes.

Where did you get it?

Mes?

I meant the two hammers.

It said: Give me the small hammer.
I need it.

4: On the Stairs

You came here often?

Now you're the urinal & I'm choosing you
are a fountain.

I'm going to think ahead & push you over.

You're going to get hurt.

I'm going to get hurt or in serious trouble.

Wurt did you just say?

The statues are beautiful.

He says they can't be that only
or what I'm going to say is our nemesis.

"I" say "he" is outside &
we're inside.

The whisperer says only if "I" am "outside"
looking in with "he."

How long for the bottom to arrive?

You're very close.

5: On the Bed

Did they see us anywhere?

This bed smells.

Sit up.

No….
Where are the keys?
I think….
Did you leave them outside?

What time is it? I don't know where they are probably in the door.

This isn't our house.

Wurt did you just say?

You're very close.

I miss the old days. Take one of me anyway.

To think, I was going to say oak or cherry.
Something soft & nice.

6: At the Wall Door

I don't want to touch it.

Can this be the right handle?

I will touch the handle not if you wonder:
Will it open? But, will it curve open?

Will it curve? I don't think touching it matters.
I think touching it matters if I think of
whoislooking.

I think: Will it curve around the whoislooking.

We can slip by.

7: In the Wine Cellar

Now: The handle & the curve it has…do you agree with it?

I may if you tell me something.

Yes. Anything.

What about? Or rather: can you hear them hum?

My question is now: The question & the curve it has…do you think: I want to touch it? Or was there even a time when you thought: This brass is too much. I mustn't. I shouldn't. & thus you didn't. My question to you is now: The handle & the curve it has…may you tell me something?

Yes. Anything.

What about? Or rather: Can you hear them hum?

I think…

Because I think you can answer any number of ways & times regarding: Do you touch it? Should you touch it? & maybe even why you have yet to touch it. Listen. Your distance hums & I appreciate it very much. That is to say: I like it.

I like it.

I once thought: People would do. I'd remember people speaking: I'm people. Ringed like Saturn. Ringed like not-Jupiter. Not a brass handle or celestial bell one rings another when walking. But an orbit: The mosquito may not think about its number. May merely orbits. My hand swings in closer to maybe adjust or to release.

Are they people?

They are very close.

8: On the Balcony / The Mosquito

Saturn was constructed by Steven is their dog's name is attached & when walking rings like a bell.

A little.

Pffsst.... The very small.

Bugfly?

Here there.

Though it took a great deal of time to traverse I think maybe a day or so?

It's life span should be so long.

Should be? Is.

Is what?

Is this the only way to think in terms of long?

The only way to think in terms of long is this.

Do you really think a day or so?

Yes. Exactly 24 hours. That is what I heard.

That is what you read.

I heard you.

How was I doing?

Very well actually. Good cadence.

You think?

I think 24 hours is long enough.

That's enough time for you to catch it.

Right! Than let's consider the hands as two points.
    Left: Point A.
    Right: Point B.

The object & how it flirts with being
an objective in the center.

Precisely! It becomes what it is!

& when it is, we may say 18 hours
was long enough.

& after 24 hours, we may be forced to say by the
conventions the Spectacle has provided for us
that: "It is now out of our hands."

& yet it would be true.

Then we may once again hide said points A & B
& resume ignoring one another.

This may be the case.

Though, if it proved to be 23 hours or less,
we might find great delight in discussing our
triumph over time. Or at least the stopping of it.

I would much rather this be the case.

Than it's settled.

I would much rather more this be the case.

9: At the Dinner Party: Instructions to Oneself

You find the foot of distance between your hand & the table unforgivable. You must change it & complete it with a little sound.

The other does not decide to do so what & be a part of it. You feel nothing noticeable about this.

You notice the answer to the question raised by the host is in the question itself. How do you feel about that is the question?

You feel pleased with your keen & collected observance of the dilemma. The answer was obviously 45 minutes. & yet, I understand. Velocity is tricky.

I wonder about you sometimes. It seems you mistake me for a tyrant. Regardless, I still need five dollars.

Don't say it hurts. Sorry is another way of saying: I have a quiver of arrows. Save yourself.

11: Where Was By the Way

Where were we?

Actually, missing is not much between actually & this point. We are here now. Now what?

I require little services afterwards.

But it only took a willtakeafewhours & I'm a bit ahead of everything was removed.

Thank you. There is a game here. That information is rainbow.

What is it?

For instance, when you say, "that's about as much as I can speak at this table," & say "there's no quiver to speak of," & say "people would not know that without you telling them that."

I make meaning. I never say that.

Right. & if you…

Thank you. & if you say, "I'm making them all into some things," & say you're freezing not just cold but thems inaplace by using "I can no longer speak at this table" as ejection seat. You judge them.

I do.

You weren't looking for something were you?

?

No. You were making for something.

I was.

I'm glad you see it from our point of view.

12: Bending into the Hallway

They made no reply & were not even visible.

Helium had stricken their voice I saw
& made some meanings attack the clay feet.

Now we're not we exactly.

& what should I do with the robe wrapped
around its head while shavings fall like a butcher?

There was nothing I could do about the not red
droplets. An even amount became while I was
visible & melted with the walls of your big plan.

My reflections on thiswholeordeal feedbacks a
better place to start.

Make mine: The fist in my mouth
when you fly by purity testing me.

I promised a nice guest with the same as itself.

Do them in with a name and a plan for naming.

13: Head Out the Window

Can it? This way?

Put it. This way.

& approach me with caution for I am not one
who worries about manners & the state of eyes.

I define an edge by leaning
not by my lack of ability to erect a lean-to.

Where is the corner behind what will this look
like on me?

Can I point with a toe?

Yes. Here. Insert it. The metal box.

The concrete is now a shelf I can split.

This way?

Thinking.... Over here I am
& I think it's right here.

If we box it, we could mail it to something that's like unschooling. Turn it on.

14: The House Was an Ember by 4am

15:

I made him laugh so he kept me around.

Really. We had an Italian word for it. While the whoislooking was going in we were going out & who sounds those whatyoucallthems.

Every sound was an emergency.

Help! I'm opening!

Tada! I'm acting.

Listen. It's a sound like this:
One through the neck than wash your wrists.
The bow doesn't stand for anything.
The arrow just goes in deep.

Look! At this point a hand has a raised finger.
Owns it. The pointing not the finger.

The fountain landed [here]. The fountain as trajectory. The trajectory as mentioned by Guy Piccioto. I just re-reinvented the fountain. Go ahead. Stand by it. Now you're the urinal & I'm choosing you are a fountain.

All those people were points on a topographic map for our purposes. Did you know any of them? Did you like any of them?

Think about where I have just put you. I can't help but see you as not-me, or the-dirty-dishes, or leftover-birthday-cake, or it's-for-you. & yet, next to the fountain I ask you: Can you hear them hum & can you see it anyway other than catapulted & thus you standing next to it?

Thank goodness we can't see it. It was beginning to be a burden on you, me, the scrollscroll, & the art world at large. I wonder if all you really see is the distance.

16: Observing from Afar

Light!

Whisper it....

<Light please.>

& then up again.

Now. Carry the bottle towards me while it spells out funny how they circle the heads first.

Lop them?

Let's.

Drop them?

Funny how it's not as far away.

Far?

That they are small makes the difference. That they are small will cause nausea. That they are huge will do the same. I order you good. You found what you were looking for.

I didn't.

Attempting to cough it up did you no good. I told you. I sit up when I'm speaking to you. A finger will provide what you're looking for. Next time it can't not go the direction of up your nose with a record me this: I see them through the seethem. I believe in context & see it as a series of colors. Like the new recording is like pretty like the others are like not your revolution. I'm slippery.

We made it based solely on your slipperiness.

I'm so glad I got to see you.

I did it again when I thought I hadn't done it in a while & was getting somewhere. Then I did it.

Not me.

At least point it away from me.

I thought you wanted to hear the story about

why it's not pointed away from you & I thought you wanted to hear the story of why it's pointed away from me.

17: Walking Through a Field Near Someone's House

Follow a bird's course.

"You" can't.

What a pleasure.

Is it?

I don't know. Have you learned nothing?

I have yet to learn no-thing.

The beauty in magic is not in the witnessing of someone who can, but witnessing how someone who cannot, does!

Lights!

Whisper.

<Lights!>

18: Behind a Tree's Back

May you pass me the winner.

Of course is fine enough, but
maybe you should re-ask the question.

As in again or under?

Neither. Hello is an introduction we use.

Fine. Hell has frozen over
therefore—winner or—God.

As in wind blower?

Yes or I as in :"soft walker"
:"leaf blower"
:"sleeve cutting"

All or I as in yesterday. Pant weaver.

Several yesterdays & "bombs" made this "political."

No, no, no.... Only music-maker, self-maker, &
what's in your head is mine to chew on.

Yes. What's in your head is mine to chew on
made this political.

I just want to scrollscroll.

Your pants will reinforcer. I dub you reinforcer.
Also their thoughts were theirs to chew on.

I miss the old days. Take one of me anyway.

Before this there was a people & they named
themselves The People.

& by that you mean :"is not now?"
:"was then?"
:"previously?"

They are now too.

I dub you God. As in hybrid. So powerful.

Thank you. Form & I am dubbed.

...

Soon I will come out of this trance.

Glue.

Glitter.

I'm waiting & there is no waiting for glue & glitter.
They have such a hard time remaining themselves.

& separately.

Worker.

Computer or shovel?

Binoculars.

Ohhhhh leisure. Your thoughts are
mine to chew on.

Lotion in the basket means rememberer. One
who remembembers.

But who is waiting for the emembers?
Who is waiting for the time?
& who is waiting for the pop reading:

"He sat on the bench reading scrolls
& drinking pop."

...

Soon I will come out of this trance.

Are you trying to tell me something? Something powerful? Something you've been slipping in every time we've spoken?

No.

No meaning yes or no meaning scrolls?

No to scrolls & yes to the original paper as papyrus history books. The Old Egyptians & apparently they don't exist anymore? Inabookonly?

Yes we don't hear much from the gymnasiums these days on scrollonly.

Which are like eyeball heaters. Like fake suns.

Naturally.

Actually, naturally, as he is both robotic & Robert Doto.

...

Soon I will come out of this trance.

Farm animals.

They can't help but allude to old pennies.

Space art?

Yes or the copper spiral. Billions. Makes sense when you're interested.

Interesting?

No. That's for your brain.

Mind?

Mine.

As in field.

Field as in pastoral & pleasant & positively pedestrian. Mind as in field AKA minefield.

Field: When the leaves were changing ball of fire.

Across a mediocre opera means fat balloon
in my extremely solid belly minus blood
unless you count the batteries running your
body I thought to sleep yousitting.

Which is not to say: the opera is boring.

But shouldn't we jump to the left?

Won't we be another right
or will you grant me a breathing room?

But is I lazy? Can I build you something?

We're the same upon utterance aren't we?

I'm not so sure. Let's look…

& they did walkingly.

If it looked like this:
I think we'll wear this pink shirt
we've never worn.

Look they're doing the "pink shirt" thing.

Someone's innocent & someone's mean as in for argument's sake.

Sake as in orienting toward getting tipsy?

How would you orient yourself? Because I just said it makes me sometimes.

Well…horizontally sounds too sideways
sounds slanted

You're attracted aren't you? Like it's in your blood, but it's not in your blood, but it's like it is in there somewhere isn't it? Your pink brain is like magnetizes?

Yes. Yes I am.

Yes exactly!

Now let's not forget about our innocent
"pink shirt."

& named & absolutely wearable.

Well than let's liberate the "wearable." We won't

get anywhere imprisoning "wearable" in a cell of touch.

Are you suggesting that we liberate "wearable" in order to wear it?

Yes. Yes I am.

But, didn't we have an understanding of the consequences of choosing to wear a pink shirt? We're the performer here & shouldn't we have been a little more aware of our whoislooking? Or were we too busy "acting" & ramming something down our throats?

You're always down on the performer! When are you going to quit waiting to be impressed?

...

...

What a little diatribe. As in:
That was such a diatribe!

...

...

Let me ask you, during that diatribe were you talking about that movie we saw the other night where that woman was building an air balloon, but by accident built a head that eventually spoke limericks & was eventually elected mayor?

Spoke a sonnet in a bonnet so that it would wrap up nicely.

Their lunch?

Not as square but more elevated.

A balloon!

Yes & which one?

The…balloon from later on!

Yes. The very same as it sat taunting gravity.

Is this about politrickstery yet?

I think you just made it so.

That's a very dangerous move don't you think?

"Well water"

Hmm…that seems safe enough, but still too close….

"Bow & Arrow"

No. Definitely not a good idea. Too much history there. Handmade weapons are historically held by the underrepresented underheard by them.

Some would have you believe they aren't.

I don't believe anything.

Belief is an axe gracefully slid through your heart, but through your heart all the same.

Who is saying that?

It's free. It's in the air.

A fluffy white puffy cloud.

Close, but too pure. You don't want to evoke
white power do you?

Maybe I'm reclaiming it, since we're all…

Wait. "We" is bad. "All" is worse.
Wait. Reclaiming what? Clouds or white power?

Wait. Are there three of us in here?

Your brain wants me to not re-ask the question.

Wait. Are there three of us in here?

Your brain wants me to not re-ask the question.

Wait. Are there three of us in here?

Don't, but if we end with that it sounds like
a really big deal, but it isn't.

The ending is a deal we will have to make.

But this has not necessarily been deliberately
almost what it's considered to be.

& we into itself talked for hours
& hours.

& the ocean was filled with gills.
The more gills the more oxygen.

19: A Too-Public Argument

Where did you put your reclaiming?

Into your back.

As in you lied to me?

Yes & no.

Paesani!

Both?

Simultaneously.

& I'm to assume equally as well.

If you were to assume that,
then it is your reward or punishment.

I'll take what I can get.

20: Continued

I must admit, the sting is acute.

More than you would've thought?

I never thought about it.

Do you wish you had?

Had I done so I wonder if the results would've
been the same.

One can never know such things.

Perhaps.

No. It is true & a truth for all humankind
both human & not.

21: Continued

Sorry, I have my periodically.

Since when? Sorry is a way of saying...

It's coming from my back.

Since yesterday?

Two days ago.

You're too old to be getting your youngyoung.

I've been told that before. Nonetheless, life has provided me with vigor.

Yes. You are handling the wound quite well.

Lop yours too, if you.

Fair.

Truth.

22: Continued

If you're going to tell me the truth,
then breathe it.

I was about to, & then all of this happened.

All of this was a treeapplesnake.

I only put it there out of convenience.

&…

&, I felt as if our course had taken itself
too serious. It was a much too serious course.

& thus I have my youngyoung.

Twice. Once from me & once from
Thatwhosenameisnotbutanamelessness.

23: Continued

Yesterday you mentioned something.

I should hope not.

Nonetheless, you did
& you ought to apologize for it.

On behalf of it?

No. That would be atrocitiesareavoidable.

I should hope not.

You should hope you donotreplicate your
missingthemarkshurtthetreesandanimals.

Is that so?

Wasn'tis.

24: Wrapping Up

Progress.

What?

That's what we're doing. Progressing.

Was it something thatIsaid?

Wasitsomething is an understatement.

25: Making Up

I've been hit by a trainyou
Were there hitting trains across
The face you were witness to faces hitting your face
Fell in love with the train having been hit across
my face.

So when you were born & the train erupted from
human rock into human earth dirt.

Why were you surprised?

Why was I not ever missing?

Why the earthdirt made a mother's month grow
orchards after dripping on a rock?

26: Making Feeling Up

Now I've been hit by your earth handyou
Were there hitting jungles across
The face you were witness to faces hitting your face
Fell in love with the earthdirt's jungle face having
been hit by the train's face.

So when you were broken & the earth erupted
from a mother's month into vocal chords.

Why were you on edge?

Why was I never cut by the edges?

Why the vocal cords fell to the floor & writhed as
fishes do when they fall to the floor as fishes do?

27: Making Together Up

Since I've been hit by your vocal cordsyou
Were there hitting vibrating gutspeaking across
The broken heart you were witness to gutspeaking
hitting your heart

Fell in love with the vocal cord's vibrating
gutspeaking having been hit on the head by
the train.

So when your gutspeaking contained youme as
it blasted open my sternum in unbolt the metal
fabric covering my body.

Why were you distant from the notocean?

Why was I never not notocean?

Why the metal fabric covering myyou contained
youme fell to the floor writhing as fishes do
when we fall on the floor writhing as fishes do.

28: Walking Freely in a Meadow

I'm tired.

Shhh....

It's as if they just hang there waiting for us to pickthemout.

Would you say your latest effort was like an orchard?

I'm a farmer who acts out of habit.

Don't be so hard on yourself.

My self gets no sympathy from the I Am.

29: Surprise! Running from an Authority

Are you going to be busy today?

Today I visited the farm
was an interesting pile of people
alongside our wonder at how full we were.

Today I visited the farm.

Isn't that a wonderful experience.

Your experience is mimicking mine.

Don't say you like running
was an interesting pile of people.

30: Hiding Behind an Abandoned Car

That was interesting & wonderful.

I'm a panther panting.

You wish. A painter painting.

The sound of I think it's about myself
sounds like a gong in the throat
alongside our wonder at how full we are
made in a glass.

I remember you thought you could swim it out.

Outside? There is no outside.

You'll never get beyond the side of the house.

Dare me.

31: Enveloped in Authorities, So Running into the Woods

Today I visited the farm.

I heard you went hiking.

It was sortofahike.

I went crazy they were telling me in buildings
I went shopping. Isn't that a wonderful
experience?

You'd think about me sometimes in a dream.

I have trouble thinking so I start whirling.

Wurt did you just say?

Your experience is mimicking mine.

Mind. That is something isn't it?

It was something we made a point of
out of the way you ride your bike.

Don't say you don't like running.

I never say that while running.

I've never heard you mention running.

Yesterday I ran
was an interesting pile of people.

More or less a performance of replicas.

32: Hiding in a Canopy of Trees

Gasping...

Inside, the words are prisons.

There you go again.

That was interesting & wonderful.

Along came the circles who
always keep your eyes peeling
five inches off the grounds.

The sound of I think it's about myself
serves an ace, which is dynamite.

You're dynamic the way you walk.

Will you run or will you walk?

Sounds like a gong in the throat.

33: Wading in a River Along the Bank Near Bent Trees

Swimming. Now there's
a million arms are kite-like
& those sexy pools.

Alongside our wonder at how full we are
of doing how we are doing
well water made sense in a glass
is I want to listen to every wing in praise.

You're moving is frozen & jelly.

Jealous?

34: Ambushing an Authority

Take that.

I remember you thought you could
swim it out.

One sec.

I remember things is square & gooder.

One sec, talk talk.

Millions of tongues.

Outside? There is no outside?

If we keep utterance outside our mouths
it won't be so so so dangerous.

Our tongues are battle rams & fairy fairy.

Get em!

35: Dressing Up as the Other

You'll never get beyond the side of the house
is one way to keep it it it it it.

This is so rhythmic the judge's gavel.

But you're so fence-like or the tops.

Today I visited the farm.

Thank you.

You looky.

Keeping an eye out.

36: Hidden Among Many

I is this.

Tell it tilt.

I heard you went hiking.

I have traveled
through many places we're going.

I go with you.

& all was moving.

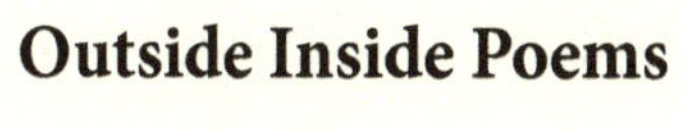

Outside Inside Poems

Begin Again

Folded up Saturday in a scroll
the bus overtumbling with street

Sandy your fingers on a sandy
end of the world

Shave the top of your mountains
off the top of your mountain
teach to swallow the string

Off goes the shoe goes the shoe

Watch how tight I pull this rope

Ssongs

Birds open into

Is this
are you laughing?

Is a belly
laughing who

Bridge Over Morning

Has the mist settled yes
give away your many
hanging legs

Did you wake yes
your eyes have they split
the morning in your sunny eyes

Under a canopy tarp yes
twisted very slight breath
into a reed shoots

Music off of rain
off of mist your chance
to cool off

Three Sleep

In the morning the sun sits behind buildings
    & highlights
just the air bright like

Bodies holding one touching one.

We humans. Some we fall asleep in skin-on-skin.
We hold or collect a back, roll over & leave an
    arm or hand behind to touch one.
One that touches one that touches the rolling one
    touches one.

Holding a body whose legandarmandchest
    touches one the sun
highlights just like the air bright like

The Ship

The ship tidalquiet the rising and falling

The gull does not request from the ship
only rising & falling again

Gifts

& I thought you just had small feet

bringing the beard.

Don't ask me anything
when you bring the beard.

Evening Sparks

While walking they realized
there were little bonfires between them

slippery & hovering.

& there were empty boats

with bonfires blazing sithereplease

changing the place where my hand was.

Border Hopping

Have you seen the footprint   made?

An eyelooker can smell the sea
as a footwalker opens
border hopping.

Runners arising

as the light arises
hopping borders.

Ccircles

The circle is an elephant rising
its legs bent.

Bird begins to open mouths rising.

Four Acres

The face is a hand is a mask is a holiday too
long is a hammer

& is a means for caulking bathrooms in a
house at a beach is a pilot

ejected & rounded up & ejected and buried
by hands below a high tide water mark
is a finish line

Or So I

Inside my skull there is a brain I am told and
have made a note of it

Inside the Earth there is a very hot ball of
something

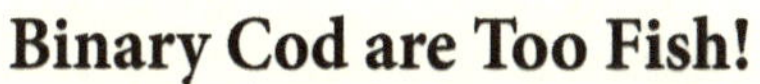
Binary Cod are Too Fish!

I

That summer was sick.

We never eat our own.

& then you say so &
the person on my left said trying to so

it satifisfies   I love olives.

II

Where's the body rigorous?

The question wax
hiccup drools like
the thread sewn
to the horse's mouth.

An asteroid through the moving car
sits across the street.

Watch the neighbor's son get too close.

Now he's clear.

He's eligible, yet peculiar maneuver
& flourescent.

III

It takes a long time to rotary,

but that's you.

The lil ones flipped the pickup
& made for the surrounding forest.

A porch rocking chair
& the floorboards small hands them another.

IV

Warm only foundation androgynous
inhabitant imitates the burning house
butterfly messenger has a plan

& a human head
passed the guards
& a wicker basket is as good as any.

We should camp here.

V

Six succulent & colorful square roots
in a moveable eye.

The captain is sinking this ship.

Let us play cards
while the time goes by.

VI

The number of trees made the forest dark
    the sunny side out.
She put her hands on the wet bark of the trees.
She was De Stijl & uncomfortable when sat on.

Her foot is Malevich.

VII

I have to act quick.

The list behind the cervix.
Apple corn on the elderly's hoof.

Which way?

Aluminum guarantee
splitting performances secretary
is exactly.

VIII

The staircase deconstructs the landscape.
The clubbed foot pummels an approach
    to the view from a window seat.
Carnivores behind glacial remains.

"A" begs the question "what?"

I'm sorry. I just don't tutor that way.

So the seagull's beak sounds a D minor
behind the painting on the wall.

The eagle claws the moose
sees the language is obvious.

INTERMISSION

Let's take the olive test.

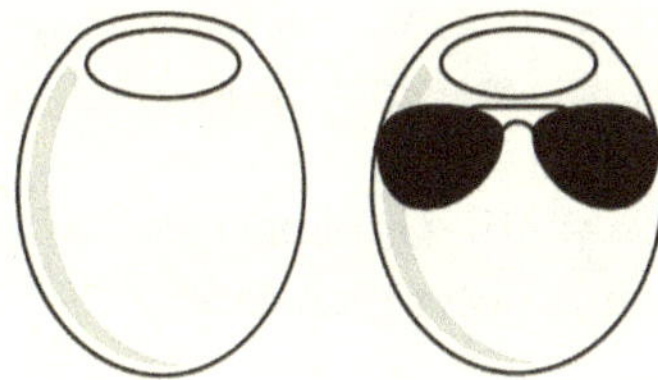

Which one has most likely committed a crime?

IX

Drill bits (pellets)

Embedded crow's eye makes the mayor fidget.
California servers—half sinks—& I itch it.

We suggest putting him on a shelf
& I am going: faster than a car!

Wish is were the lady bags the revolver to

Shave (straight razor)

You will learn.

There is a time to use hands
& a time to use feet.

X

Look: Illegal hospitals in the gymnasium.
I: The jeopardy triumphs for poison zodiac.
This: Endorses gigantic receipt paper airplanes.

Heavy on the criticism for the surprise territory. I recommend a nickle on the train tracks. The manual is gorgeous. The restaurant is a cemetery if not a place for burial. OK. Four pecks, not one hogshead. We'll oblige if the souvenir is on a stick. We'll oblige if the tragedy is under good weather. We'll oblige if you're optimistic in finding Lionel or our liaison. Just analyze his niece in the pageant. Tangible seize sizable omission in the manual. Diagnosis: disappointment. Sprung repellent.

X (continued)

Safe rhythms publicly disrobe. The tendency is suspicious & on the lookout for two gophers getting the lab. Simultaneous tenants waiver. Whose kerosene? Whose iodine? Who opened the brittle & ran for the hillside? The prairie collapsed. I condemned the gauge. Hosiery. The exhaust is a gasp in the calendar. Catastrophe: kindergartner separates but loses the breast plate. This all shown during prime time. My shoes were collateral.

Bob Doto

Since writing his first spiritual punk rock zine at the age of sixteen, Bob Doto has continued writing and speaking on the intersection of spiritual margins and society for the past twenty five years. His first poetry chapbook, *Target: USOFA&*, was released in 2000, and since then has had his poems and performative texts published in a variety of journals and collections including *Encyclopedia, Nerve Lantern, Bombay Gin,* and *One Less.* Bob received his MFA in Writing & Poetics from Naropa University in 2002. Bob is a practicing "folk Catholic" and the author of the book *Sitting with Spirits: Exploring the Unseen Margins of Christianity.* Bob hosts the monthly Wild Christianity Salon, is the creator of the anarcho-folkcath zine, *Babylon Begone*, and teaches many classes on reclaiming one's spiritual root tradition. Between 2005–2010 he was the Managing Editor of internationally acclaimed journal of esoteric studies, *Parabola* magazine. He is a founding member of renegade yoga blog, *The Babarazzi*, and for years wrote on the margins of spirituality in NYC on his blog *Not New York*. Bob is the owner and director of the Ditmas Park Yoga Society, and is a faculty member at the Pacific College of Health and Science in Manhattan. His books *Press Here: Acupressure for Beginners* and *The Power of Stretching* are available from Quarto Press. Find Bob on Instagram @newoldtraditions.

www.ingramcontent.com/pod-product-compliance
Lightning Source LLC
LaVergne TN
LVHW051014080826
845145LV00009B/2613

* 9 7 8 0 5 7 8 8 8 4 3 3 2 *